FOREWORD

Originality or non-confirmity is maligned as madness by those whose vested interests are affected by any changes in thinking and action. Gora does not feel shy of calling himself an atheist and for over four decades has been carrying on an active campaign for the cause of atheism. His opponents called him " mad" and his friends advised him to drop atheism as it was a 'lost cause' and an 'unpopular creed,' so that he might be accepted in higher circles. But Gora's life-mission is to propagate and popularise atheism, in spite of the odium attached to it through prejudice and misunderstanding. He believes in individual freedom, the basis of democracy. He considers god a falsehood and holds religion responsible for dividing humanity into fragments. He stands for the removal of social and economic inequalities which are perpetuated by the exploiters and tolerated by common believers in the name of god and religion. He spells "god" with a small letter to treat it as a 'capital' falsehood without any holiness.

Gora was an intimate and close associate of Mahatma Gandhi and worked with Vinoba Bhave. He is in the mainstream of the national politics and is connected with all reform movements in India for the removal of caste and religion. In this booklet it is my intention to present briefly Gora and his work in the right perspective. As a thinker, rationalist, humanist and above all atheist, Gora stands prominently as a man devoted to a non-violent revolution in society. He is not an arm-chair thinker but he carries on many campaigns on political, social and economic fronts. The name GORA gives a shock to many Indians. Though people disagree with him, they do not doubt his sincerity. Perhaps in their heart of hearts there is a lurking fear, "After all Gora may be right." If Gora is right, god does not exist. Consequently the intellectual situation is puzzling to the believers.

Gora proposes atheism as a corrective to Gandhism and Marxism, the former lacking any stress on the importance of the political action in bringing about changes in society and the latter with its philosophy of class struggle based on hatred and violence and its totalitarian tendencies. He stands for partyless and pompless democracy. His views are not confined to the Indian situation only but they have a relevance to any human situation. He insists that one should regard oneself as a human without any label, religious, political or national. He has inspired many people with his views. I hope that this booklet will be of interest to all those who are eager to know the changing society in India and the part Gora and his co-workers are playing in bringing about those changes in their own sphere.

At the end, an article by Mr. Bjorn Merker (of Sweden) from Peace News, *London, is given with a few extracts from Gora's writings to help the reader have a direct access to some of his views on atheism, democracy and economic equality.*

Atheistic Centre,
  Vijayawada-6,
    (India).
                              G. S. RAO.

GORA – AN INTRODUCTION

In the early hours of the morning on the 30th March 1945 an unassuming visitor met Mahatma Gandhi in his *ashram* at Sevagram. He felt as if he were sitting by the side of his father to consult him closely on a domestic affair. The visitor said, in the course of his wide-ranging discussion, "God is a falsehood conceived by man. Like many falsehoods, it was, in the past, useful to some extent. But like all falsehoods, it polluted life in the long run. So belief in god can go and it must go in order to wash off corruption and to increase morality in mankind. I want atheism to make man self-confident and to establish social and economic equalities non-violently. Tell me, *Bapu*, where I am wrong." Bapu (as Gandhi was affectionately called) listened to him patiently and replied slowly : "Yes. I see an ideal in your talk. I can neither say my theism is right nor your atheism wrong. We are all seekers after truth. We change whenever we find ourselves in the wrong. I changed like that many times in my life. I see you are a worker. You are not a fanatic. You will change whenever you will find yourself in the wrong. There is no harm as long as you are not fanatical. Whether you are in the right or I am in the right, results will prove. Then I may go your way or you may come my way, or both of us may go a third way. So go ahead with your work. I will help you, though your method is against mine." The visitor was more than satisfied with Gandhi's reply. He is Gora who has been bold enough to call himself an atheist.

Had Gandhi lived longer he would have performed Gora's eldest daughter's marriage to a so-called untouchable at his own *ashram*. It would have been the first of its kind according to Gandhi's wishes. He was even willing to substitute the word "god" with "truth" as Gora protested against the use of the word god in the wedding of an atheist.

BIRTH AND CHILDHOOD

Just as in ancient India the name "Charvaka" was synonymous with atheism so in modern India is the name "Gora". It is a person's name formed from the first two letters of his full name in Telugu "Goparaju Ramachandra Rao". Born in an orthodox Hindu Brahmin family on November 15, 1902 at Chatrapur, a small town in Orissa State, he was brought up on traditional lines. His father was a government officer and a well-known theist and composer of devotional songs. Gora's early life bore the mark of theistic training under his father.

Gora's early education was at Kakinada, a famous town in Andhra. At the age of nineteen he married Saraswathi, aged eleven, a daughter of his father's friend. It was an arranged marriage. After the marriage, he went to Madras for higher studies at the Presidency College. In 1925 he took the Master's degree in Botany.

ATHEIST IN THE MAKING

After his university education Gora was appointed a lecturer in Biology at the American College, Madurai, in the Madras Presidency. It was there that he had an opportunity to lead a free life without the shackles of tradition and parental authority. He put traditional beliefs to a severe test in his life. He rented, without fear, a house supposed to have been haunted by ghosts. The rent was cheap, since for a long time nobody had dared to occupy it, although the landlord offered it for a lower rent. Gora stayed alone in that spacious house and gradually others joined him. Thus his scientific thinking and training of the mind on modern lines helped him to expose the shallowness of the belief in ghosts. Thus he could repudiate other superstitions as well.

As a teacher he devised new ways of teaching. He paid individual attention to and instilled confidence in the students. He opposed stoutly the out-worn system of detaining students from appearning for the public examinations and insisted that all students should be sent up for the examination. He removed the fear of the examination from the minds of the students by keeping himself in close contact with them and helping them to the outmost. Gora's students did well at the examinations and the fears of the College authorites were belied.

Gora's moral principles were put to a test at this college. The college authorities offered him a chance to go to the United States for higher studies. But they laid down a condition that he should convert himself to Christianity. Gora was not willing to change his religion to avail himself of this rare opportunity in life. Even then he seriously doubted the existence of god and ruled out change of religion though one is as good or as bad as another.

Gora spent a year in cotton research on the Government Agricultural Farm at Coimbatore. His young wife joined him there and was initiated into scientific outlook on life. She was till then under the influence of orthodox Hindu tradition but could now appreciate her husband's views and co-operate with him in his adventurous search and fight for truth. Gora made a comparative study of Hinduism and Christianity. His independent study of religions without the assistance of a religious guide, or a *guru*, as is enjoined on the searchers of truth by the Hindu scriptures, led his mind into non-conformist and rationalist paths. He resigned his Government job as he could noι fit into the dull routine of the official duties. His resignation came as a shock 'o the members of is family as in those days a Government job was coveted and promised security and was a symbol of prestige.

WAR ON SUPERSTITIONS

From Coimbatore Gora went to Ceylon to take up a teaching job at Ananda College, Colombo, a Buddhist institution. It was here that he came into contact for the first time with an alien culture. Though Buddhism had its birth in India it migrated to other lands. As its influence was not felt perceptibly in the place of his bir.h, to Gora it was alien. What shocked him most at Colombo was the wide gulf between the profession and the practice of Buddhism. The Buddhist priests who controlled the administration of the college objected to Gora's work in the laboratory when he wanted to dissect a frog to show its heart-beat to his students. The Buddhist priests considered the dissection of the frog as wilful killing, which is contrary to the basic moral principles taught by Buddha, though they ate meat from animals slaughtered by a butcher. Gora was shocked at and amused by the behaviour of the Buddhist authorities over their compassion for animal life, which differed from their practice. How can biology be taught without dissection of animals? Mere teaching of theory without experimentation will not do justice to the study of a scientific subject. This was an instance of Gora's upholding of truth even if it brought him into conflict with the authorities. At Sevagram also years later Gandhi's orthodox followers objected to Gora's dissection of a frog when he taught student-nurses. But Gandhi allowed Gora to dissect the frog for the purpose of scientific demonstration and did not consider it an outrage against his creed of non-violence.

Gora's mind dwelt on the blind religious superstitions and wanted to expose them by subjecting them to scientific test. He wrote articles in Telugu, his mother-tongue, for the sake of readers who did not have the benefit of modern education and could not read English. His articles were thought-provoking and revolutionary, and challenged traditional beliefs and customs.

Gora's ideas were not intended merely for the public at large. He taught his wife at home, who cooperated with him in conducting experiments which would shock the common folk. It was a superstitious belief among the pregnant Hindu women that they should not cut vegetables or move about during the period of an eclipse. They would be confined to bed as it was believed that the slightest movement would bring about physical deformity of the child in the womb. Gora and his wife asked themselves why this belief was confined only to the Hindus while the Muslims and the Buddhists were free from it. What is true should be equally and universally valid for all religions and in all climes. So Gora encouraged his wife, who was with child to cut vegetables, move about and indulge in all activities prohibited by Hindu custom. The eldest child was born without any physical deformity to the utter dismay of the old women of the family who disapproved of this fool· hardiness in the young couple. Gora's social reforms and scientific exposure of superstitions started at home with the active and the whole-hearted cooperation of his wife, unlike the case of many reformers and thinkers who preach to others without practising their beliefs at home. In this context it should be said that to Gora his wife is an asset and without her help his propaganda against superstitions among women might not have much headway. The example of his wife inspired many women to free themselves from the shackles of blind belief and superstition.

EDUCATOR AND SOCIAL REFORMER

Gora resigned his job in Ceylon in 1928 and came back to his native town Kakinada to serve P. R. College of which he was an old student. With revolutionary notions about caste and religion he inspired the students to think and act on original lines. With a band of student volunteers he organised a campaign against untouchability, visited the slums and conducted adult education classes. He believed that without education and enlightenment untouchability could not be removed. His frequent visits to *Harijan* (untouchable) hamlets brought him into clash with the orthodox members of his family who, raising their high brows, said that Gora broke the rules of caste by sitting and dining with the untouchables.

To add fuel to the fire of their ire against Gora, he removed the sacred thread which a Brahmin must wear as a symbol of his high caste. Gora would consider himself a human being without any caste label. He expressed his unorthodox opinions strongly. He desired to give and take no more respect than is due to a man as man without any complex of social superiority. This attitude to life based on equal respect for all infuriated his elders and he was outcast from the family fold. It was only years afterwards that they were reconciled to him in the changed social conditions in the country.

Continuing as a lecturer at the college, Gora contributed his mite to the movement for independence in 1930. He recruited volunteers to take part in salt satyagraha, that is, defiance of bans imposed by the Government on the manufacture of salt. He discarded the western form of dress and attended the college in *Khadi* (hand spun hand woven cloth). The college authorities insisted that all those wearing national dress should put on turbans. His students came in turbans much to the surprise of the authorities. Later they withdrew the restrictions on dress. Gora took away the odium attached to national dress at a time when western dress, customs and manners were held in high esteem and were considered symbols of prestige. In wearing the national dress Gora could mix with the common people easily. Even now he wears this simple dress.

Gora helped the poor students. Students in general used to visit his house, take their meals there and discuss matters of moment. In addition to their studies they had the benefit of knowing Gora's views on social reform. He was an able and popular teacher. The students liked his teaching and views on life and respected him. Inspired by Gora's example they cultivated self-discipline. The college authorities were imbued with old notions about discipline. They insisted the teacher should teach his lessons and do nothing more and should not mix with his students but keep at a distance from them. Gora did not conform to these rigid norms but blazed a new trail of his own.

THE FIRST CONFRONTATION

In 1932 Gora spoke at a seminar on idolatry and exposed the irrationality of such worship. He said that god was merely a concept, not a scientific fact and that such a discussion seemed as absurd as a debate on the depth of water in a mirage. He wrote an article on "the concept of God" in a student magazine exploding the belief in god. He said that it was not a scientific fact but a figment of imagination, that people should feel free and strive for the removal of poverty and human suffering and that such endeavour was not possible without freeing the mind from the shackles of blind faith in god. Man should realise that he is the master of his own destiny and human happiness can be achieved only through recognition of the importance of human will and action in life which are wrongly and blindly believed to be controlled by a non-existent god.

Gora came into conflict with the college management for his atheistic views. They were afraid that Gora would corrupt the young minds and so dismissed him from service. Gora took up the matter with the then vice-chancellor of the Andhra University, Dr. S. Radhakrishna, who later became the President of India.

His plea was that students should have freedom of thought and without such freedom education was useless. For a year he was out of employment but ran a tutorial institution. He conducted an experiment in egalitarianism. He and all other teachers received equal pay for their work. Students were dedicated to their studies and to the ideals which Gora placed before them. He was free to experiment with his own ideas and welcomed this change in his life.

In 1934 Gora accepted the offer of the post of a lecturer at the Hindu College, Machilipatnam of the same university. While in service at this college Gora made attempts to start a college at a town with the help of two rich people. One of them died while the other laid down a condition that Gora should wear the sacred thread, symbolic of status as a Brahmin, if he was to receive from him a handsome sum, about sixty thousand rupees, as financial aid. But Gora made it plain that he could not compromise his principles and that honest differences of opinion should not come in the way of an educational project. It had to be given up on this account and was yet another example of the clash between traditional and progressive ways of thinking.

PERSISTENT PROPAGANDA

In 1936 Gora actively took up propaganda for atheism. He visited villages and explained to the illiterate people the need for adopting a scientific attitude to life and for giving up superstitions. His students organised those meetings. His audiences ranged from university professors and students to uneducated villagers and untouchables. People attended his meetings in large numbers to listen to "godless"

Gora. Orthodox people were unnerved by the boldness of this atheist and did not spare pains to disturb his meetings, sometimes even by throwing old shoes at him. Once a furious fanatic threw a slipper at Gora when he was addressing a large gathering on atheism. Gora took it coolly and asked the angry man to throw the other slipper also as the one without the other would be useless to either. The whole audience burst into laughter and later the angry man apologised. Gora encountered misguided opposition with superb calmness that surprised the disturbers. Gora refused to be provoked. A special feature of these meetings which went on for hours on end was that Gora devoted more time to answering questions than to his speech. He tried his best to convince them. Those who were convinced of atheism followed his teachings and like him discarded caste symbols and dined with people of other castes. They were also excommunicated like Gora but they bore troubles with calm patience.

Gora was very punctual in his attendance at public meetings. Once he began to address a public meeting with only two or three listeners at the fixed hour. Many thought that the meeting would commence late and so were late for the meeting. He told them that he liked to keep his word and would not think of wasting others time by being unpunctual. He asserted that atheism meant punctuality, that is keeping one's time and word. Thus, he taught the villagers a valuable lesson in punctuality.

Gora used to give apt and humorous replies without wounding others' feelings even though impudent questions were hurled at him. Once he was asked why he should not slap a man on his face instead of greeting him with folded hands in the traditional manner. Quick came Gora's retort that greetings were a reciprocal affair and as he was not prepared to be slaped he would not slap others.

Gora again clashed with the college authorities who imposed restrictions upon his addressing meetings. He had to choose between service to his family and himself and service to the cause of atheism. He preferred the latter as his heart was in it and resigned his job. He was then, a father of six children. He took an irrevocable decision which his wife supported. This marks the end of Gora's career as a teacher whose ability, earnestness and popularity had won him high regard throughout Andhra Pradesh.

GRASS ROOTS

Atheists at Mudunur, a village about thirty miles from the town of Machilipatnam invited Gora and his family to settle down there and to make it the centre of his activities. Gora accepted that invitation and lived there for seven years. He carried on an active propaganda for atheism. He conducted inter-caste and inter-religious dinners on a mass scale. Everybody brought his or her own provisions and cooking and dining was done on a cosmopolitan basis.

Gora had a difficult time in organising inter-caste dinners. Among Hindus inter-caste dining is prohibited. Some people, even among the untouchables, were prepared to dine with higher castes but were not willing to dine with lower castes. In this regard, Gora appealed to the lower castes to do away with social inequalities even among themselves when thinking of claiming equality with higher castes. He said that all castes from the highest to the lowest should go without any mental reservations in the best interests of social equality.

Gora once dined with a Muslim in Delhi. He was served beef. Gora ate it without a protest but asked the Muslim whether he would eat pork. The Muslim said in surprise that he would not eat pork as it was contrary to Islam. Gora said that to remove Hindu-Muslim differences changes should be brought about in age-old eating habits, Hindus and Muslims should eat beef and pork in common as both are prohibited by Hinduism and Islam respectively. Gora's outspokenness shocked the Muslim.

SPREAD OF SCIENTIFIC OUTLOOK

Gora encouraged inter-caste marriages to bring about social equality. Though contrary to custom, widow remarriages were encouraged by him. He supported the right of women to take part in the public affairs of the country and to be educated. He was the object of a slanderous campaign as he took up the cause of unmarried mothers. He encouraged them to face the problem with courage and self-confidence.

Gora ran a school for adults and taught all the advanced subjects in the mother tongue. Seminars and discussions were employed contrary to the traditional system of education. They attracted adults who later distinguished themselves in several fields.

Gora lost no opportunity to fight against superstitions. Once a palm tree grew up with a few branches near a village. The illiterate and superstitious people ascribed divine powers to it and began to worship it.

Gora explained this freak of nature scientifically. Consequently, a few overzealous atheists cut it down to prove the hollowness of the superstitious belief, much to the dismay and anger of the ignorant folk.

Mrs. Gora did not lag behind her husband in spreading the scientific spirit among village women. She organised a public demonstration of pregnant women breaking all taboos during an eclipse. All of the children were born without any physical deformities, much to the surprise of the villagers.

Gora with a band of bold workers walked on fire to demonstrate that there was nothing occult or mysterious about it and disproved the belief among the Hindus and Muslims that a fire-walker was under divine inspiration. These fire-walking demonstrations attracted large crowds. Some among them were so imbibed with scientific spirit that they walked with Gora on fire. He gave a scientific explanation to fire-walking, saying that the presence of water-vapour between the foot and the fire prevented blistering.

Once a believer entered into a discussion with Gora over the existence of ghosts. Gora disproved it and said that he would go to a cremation ground with him and that if he saw the ghost he would shoot and kill it. The believer was dismayed at Gora's fearlessness and was too diffident to take up Gora's challenge. Gora has examined problems with an impartial and open mind. Thus he exposed blind beliefs among ignorant people and exhorted them to adopt the scientific method of enquiry, observation and evaluation.

Breaking the traditional practice of naming children after gods, goddesses and ancestors Gora gave significant names to his children. His eldest son was *Lavanam* (salt) born in 1930 when Gandhi started the nation-wide Civil Disobedience campaign against Salt Laws. Lavanam follows his father's way and has been most active in the atheist movement, next to his father. He married out of caste the daughter of Joshua, one of the foremost of Telugu poets. Another of Gora's sons is *Samaram* (war) born in 1939 at the time of the outbreak of the Second World War. Thus the names of all the nine children are connected with and symbolise national and international events.

Gora as usual carried on his campaign against untouchability. He promoted the cause of public sanitation. He exhorted people to build latrines in villages. His constructive activities had much in common with Gandhiji's. So he was drawn towards the National Movement in its fight for political freedom against the British imperialist government. In 1942 Gora, his wife, eldest daughter and sister with many of his friends were arrested and imprisoned for their participation in the Civil Disobedience Movement. Gora's fight against social tyranny and exploitation thus extended to the political sphere also.

FIRST BOOK ON ATHEISM

Gora felt the need to systematise his thoughts and to give a shape to them in the form of a book. The result was his book on Atheism in Telugu, perhaps the first, in any Indian language. It was published in 1941 with financial aid provided by his friends. His main programme for socializing is inter-marriages. Three of his children married out of caste and this created a stir among orthodox people.

CONTACT WITH GANDHI

In September, 1941, Gora wrote to Gandhi asking for an interview. His intention was to know Gandhiji's opinions on atheistic programmes and philosophy. Gora wrote :

For one year I have tackled the problem of untouchability with the atheistic outlook. I have a few co-workers who agree with me in the atheistic approach. The atheistic approach mainly consists in the non-recognition of sectarian lables like Hindu, Muslim and Christian. We take man as man. Thus by discarding the lables and mixing up people in the general stream of humanity, we hope to remove untouchability also.

Our programme of work so far has been confined to systematic and periodical cosmopolitan dinners in which the guests pay for their fare which is always simple and cheap. The dinner is open to all and about forty to fifty guests, drawn from all castes including 'untouchables', take part in the dinner. The persons vary from time to time.

In the village atmosphere where caste restrictions continue to be rigid, open cosmopolitan dinners are not easy to accomplish. Yet we succeed, because we find that the atheistic attitude brings definite cosmopolitan outlook and pushes out all sectarianism including untouchability.

The results of one year's work encouraged us to proceed along the same lines. Before we do so, we desire to seek your advice. All of us have great regard for your wisdom and experience. We want to be told and warned of the possible pitfalls, if any, that lie

3

in the way of our atheistic approach. In the light of your advice we are prepared to revise our outlook and programmes. If you like, I will go to Sevagram for a personal talk with you.

Gandhiji replied :

Atheism is a denial of self. No one has succeeded in its propagation. Such success you have attained is due to your sincere work among the people round you. I am sorry I cannot invite you to come here. I have no time to spare for talks.

For two years Gora had to wait to get a favourable response from Gandhi for an interview. It was the result of his persistent efforts to meet Gandhi. As soon as they met, they understood each other. This friendly contact continued till Gandhji's death in 1948. There was a frank exchange of views which Gora recorded in *An Atheist with Gandhi* published in 1951.

IN INDEPENDENT INDIA

In 1947 Gora shifted the centre of his activities from Mudunur to Patamata near Vijayawada in Andhra. He started a weekly paper in Telugu to propagate his ideas and programmes. It was named *Sangham* (Society). All the members of his family and his friends made it a co-operative enterprise and with dynamic enthusiasm it held the field for a decade inspite of severe opposition. When there was terrible political oppression in his state, Gora through *Sangham* championed the cause of Civil Liberties. Reading of the paper was considered blasphemy but whoever read it could not but come under the sway of the revolutionary philosophy of atheism. Gora has proved that good without god is possible and has tried to remove prejudice against atheism. Even those who disagreed with atheism respected the moral behaviour of atheists.

After the assassination of Gandhiji Gora dissociated himself from the activities of the Congress party. He fell out with Gandhians who stressed the religious and spiritual aspects of Gandhism and ignored the dynamic aspects of nonviolent revolution. He carried on campaigns for partyless and pompless democracy and conducted *satyagraha* (non-violent resistence) on several occasions against ministers and governors protesting against their pompous living in the midst of poverty. He has fought against social injustices and economic inequalities.

Gora contested in elections twice as an independent candidate – in 1952 in the first general election to the Parliament and in 1967 to the State Assembly. He lost both the elections but he propagated his views on partylessness and pomplessness without any compromise.

REVOLUTIONARY HUMANISM

Gora published *Gram Raj* in 1958 in which he advocated devolution of political power and decentralisation of economy in keeping with the Gandhian ideals. *Partyless Democracy* published in 1961, condemns the parliamentary democracy based on the party system. Gora believes that democracy should be divested of political parties if it is to be living and dynamic and to serve the interests of the people. He condemns the party bosses who appropriate power to themselves and control the party machinery to exploit the people for their selfish ends. Gora was intimately connected with Indian Rationalists and Humanists and their journal *Indian Rationalist* edited by the late S. Ramanathan. Once *The Indian Rationalist* conducted a thought-provoking and interesting discussion on "Gora Puzzle". In January 1969 Gora started a monthly in English *The Atheist* to carry his views to a wider public. In January 1970 an "Atheists' Meet" was organised, the first of its kind in the world. It considered several programmes of action based on the philosophy of atheism.

In a symposium recently conducted in Vijayawada, Gora said : "If god is not already dead, kill him." He maintains that man develops only when we banish the god-idea and come out of the shell of slave-mind and assert our individuality and freewill.   His views are now received calmly and respectfully.   His meetings are no longer disturbed by fanatics as in the past. The reaction among the people is that Gora has something to say which deserves careful consideration and that his words ring with sincerity and cannot be untrue.

Gora insists on practice. "One should do what one says and say what one does." Secrecy and violence have no place in his programmes. He makes a radical scientific and humanistic approach to the problems of life without any limitations of caste, religion, party or even nationality. They are not to be judged only in the Indian context but are valid to any people for their revolutionary humanism.

GORA'S ACTIVITIES

BY

BJORN MERKER

Mr. Merker is a peace worker from Sweden. In 1964-65 he worked with various Gandhian groups in India. This service he did at his own initiative, in place of compulsory military service for the Swedish government. He spent a little over five months at the Atheistic Centre with Gora and his family studying and observing their activities. Merker describes Gora's activities in this article which was originally published in "Peace News" dated 23rd April 1965.

At the latest (1964) all-India Sarvodaya meeting, held in the South (of India), one of the very active workers started a report about local activities with: "As you know, we believe in *Satyagraha* ". Almost sounding like an apology, this statement illustrates the minority position within Sarvodaya held by advocates of what in the west goes by the name of "direct action". It has been left to a few devotees of non-violent action to try to apply the techniques developed during the freedom struggle to the social and economic problems mounting all about them in Independent India.

One of the most insistent protagonists of this minority view is a man called Gora. He believes in the establishment of the non-violent society of Gandhi's conception, but has no illusions that this can be brought about in one all-embracing transformation. He paints no beautiful utopias, but looks for revolutionary challenges at the stark facts of life around him. The revolution through a "change of heart" has to be vested in the future; Gora wants to accomplish this revolution here and now, by direct action transforming specific social conditions and practices.

Gora sees "enlightened anarchy" as a main feature of the non-violent society where the people's self-restraint and voluntary action replaces state power and coercion. This goal is brought nearer by involving people increasingly in tackling their own problems and making democracy increasingly "direct". In the present Indian context the political parties are seen as an obstacle, acting as divisive 'middle-men' between the people and their governments; Gora is critical of pomp and extravagance of Indian legislators, which create a widening gulf between them and the people. So Gora leads a direct action movement against 'party and pomp', besides carrying on constructive work in his village in Andhra Pradesh. This direct action movement is in a sense a direct continuation of the freedom struggle, in asmuch as it tries to bring about the real liberation of the common man which Gandhi saw as the goal of the non-violent endeavour.

AFTER INDEPENDENCE

Freedom did not come to the common man on the transfer of power in 1947; the supposed representatives of poverty-stricken millions began clothing themselves in extravagance and pomp much in the manner of the former colonial rulers. They now draw salaries of 500 rupees a month plus daily allowances of 31 rupees, while most men struggle to earn even *one* rupee a day. A cabinet minister draws 60,000 rupees a year plus free house, water, electricity and furniture worth 36,000 rupees. Whereas Gandhi, in identification with the common man, received foreign dignitaries on the floor in his mud hut in the sweepers' colony in Delhi, now even the cheif ministers of the various states have to inhabit palacial residences with concrete driveways for visiting cars; this does little to make the bare-footed Indian feel the advent of democracy. Lavish ministerial dinners are attended by "the servants of the people" arriving by free first-class train travel or air travel, while the farmer struggles on foot or at best in a bullock cart.

Democracy cannot function with representatives who in their very mode of living are alienated from the people they are supposed to represent, and a non-violent social order cannot be established on the large-scale social and economic inequalities which these conditions reflect. Gandhi once said: "The contrast between the palaces of New Delhi and the miserable hovels of the poor labouring class nearby cannot last one day in free India in which the poor will enjoy the same power as the richest in the land.", but he has been belied in a frightening manner. The poor have never discovered the significance of independence. They remained in their mud huts untouched by the light of changed circumstances. In theory they are free but in practice apathetic. Therefore the crusade against pomp.

But some woke up: the power-mongers and status-seekers. The political party became a vehicle for self-seeking exploits in the game of power-politics. While the mounting economic problems were crying for a solution in a spirit of national unity, much energy, money and time were spent on getting into power, remaining there or throwing others out of it.

Every party, with the words "democracy" and "service" on its lips, used the ignorant and inexperienced people merely as vote reserve to back up their factional party quarrels; situations result, such as that in Kerala, where politics are chronically unstable and float on a sea of unsolved problems. Where the problems are fundamental human ones, like lack of food and shelter, incessant party quarrells should be regarded as a criminal waste. Thus the crusade against party blocs and whips.

'CONTROL THE GOVERNMENT'

So Gora began weeding, besides nursing local constructive work. With the slogan, "Come close to the common man", he called on legislators and ministers to shed pomp and luxurious living in order to become true instruments in the cause of the suffering masses; and with the slogans, "Ministers are our servants, the people are their masters" and "Control the government", he called on the people to realise their democratic strength and come out of their apathy, to insist that their so-called representatives do their duty to the people. In the light of prevailing apathy and indolence the stress was on *satyagraha*, not only "if necessary", but *as* necessary for solving the problems of the nation.

So in the course of the 1950's Gora set about building up a nucleus of trained workers and generating public awareness on the issues; some of the early attempts were encouraging. One of Gora's demands was that ministers should travel third class on the railways as a token gesture of democratic spirit and identification with the masses. At Vijayawada railway station, a major junction not far from Gora's village, ministers needed help from the police to enter their comfortable first class compartments, clearing away the satyagrahis bodily obstructing the carriage doors while crowds of usually timid Indians shouted: "Ministers should travel third class." The practical results of these campaigns were negligible, but the psychological change they brought about in the people was profound, accomplishing the much-needed turn from submissive weakness.

More tangible results were shown in the form of a bill cutting the salaries of ministers from 1,000 to 500 rupees a month, passed by the Andhra Legislative Assembly. It was later-nullified, as the Governor did not lend it his support; but the Governor voluntarily cut his own salary by one fifth in appreciation of Gora's campaign. Six members of the Assembly joined the movement, voluntarily cutting their salaries and travelling third class only. Due to Gora's efforts, there are in India legislators advocating the abolition of the very party system which helped them into power.

Then came an opportunity to try satyagraha among the poorest of the poor. In Gora's immediate neighbourhood, hundreds of "untouchable" families were living in primitive huts on the holdings of their former employers. The land changed owners and the "untouchables" were asked to vacate it immediately. They were doing unskilled labour in the nearby town, earning not even enough to feed their families one adequate meal a day. Eviction would have sent them onto the roads and led them to starvation. The government, entangled in legalities, upheld the eviction and refused to grant any compensation or to provide alternative living space for the homeless.

After pleading their case in vain the untouchables came to Gora, whose appeals to the authorities were as futile as those of his downtrodden brothers. Gora then led the desperate families to a little used public road, and marked off a strip on one side; with combined efforts hundreds of enthusiastic homeless of all ages started erecting their huts on this strip of public land. The government called out police to clear away the ' invaders ' ; but the police met, not frightened "untouchables", but a wall of united and courageous "unbendables", under the leadership of Gora protecting their huts with their lives.

In the course of the years, as the evictions continued, with luxurious private residences rising on the former untouchable settlement, some 500 families have been settled on public land with the help of satyagraha. The fight with the government continues, now at the ministerial level, but the authorities know that forcible evictions of the "encroachers" will be met by determined satyagraha; the untouchables have been instilled with a new sense of dignity and manhood. They no longer excuse themselves, but know that they are men with as great a right to a home of their own as any minister or landlord. This is shown not only in their attitudes, but in the immaculate whitewash on the mud walls of their straw-roofed huts. It is the spirit of Satyagraha that has given them this new sense of dignity, and it is hard to see why this kind of experiment should not be tried on a wider scale for the uplift of the exploited masses.

MARCH ON THE CAPITAL

By the end of the 1950's the movement, now called Satyagraha Samaj (Direct Action Brotherhood) had created a platform and following of its own, with a core of devoted and well trained satyagrahis. With these, a 250-mile March was launched to the state capital, Hyderabad, demanding that legislators be recognised as representatives of their constituencies only and not of any party, and that blocs and whips in the Legislative Assembly be abolished. This would require a change only in conventions, and would be a first step towards an increase in the people's power and self-management.

With this objective, and after fruitless attempts at securing agreement from the Speaker of the House, the march was launched, with the intention of ending it on the floor of the Assembly, and obstructing its business. Gora and his batch of resisters were arrested upon completing the march, but before reaching the Assembly building. The Speaker informed the House about Gora's demands; they expressed agreement, but wanted an initiative from the Central Government in the matter.

This led to the 1100-mile march, headed by Gora, from Gandhiji's hut at Sevagram to Nehru's palatial official residence at Delhi. The two demands were that Nehru move into the quarters of regular members of Parliament and that he consider the abolition of party blocs and whips in the legislatures. The march generated great enthusiasm on its way, all its expenses being met by contributions from the common people, and new volunteers joining the march on its trek to Delhi.

It was obvious that the people grasped its message. Even in the backward hill regions inhabited by aboriginal tribes, illiterate people proudly exclaimed :

"Yes, one thing we understand, the ministers are our servants." This means a tremendous change of attitude among people who have been seen to tremble at the sight of the lowest district official on duty. With the banners: "People's representatives! end parties, shed pomp", "Ministers are our sarvants, the people arc their masters" and "Control the government" the protesters triumphantly entered Delhi on the 99th day of marching.

In the absence of any reply to the appeals to Nehru in his "combined capacity as the heir of Mahatma Gandhi and as the Prime Minister of India", some forty of the marchers conducted a protest picket at his residence; it was terminated on the Prime Minister's assurance of talks with Gora. The talks were held, but with no concrete results, confirming Gora in his determination to continue the movement, working from the bottom upwards.

FURTHER PROTESTS

More recent campaigns were conducted in the form of round-the-clock protest picketing of the official residence of the Chief Minister of Andhra State, demanding that he move to the regular legislators' quarters. Gora and nine satyagrahis, including three women, squatted for five days and nights before the gates of the residence. Initially the women obstructed the passage of cars through the gates, but were dragged away by police.

This protest received a wave of sympathy from all over the state, finally leading the Chief Minister to assure his efforts for evolving an all-India pattern of "pomplessness". This promise was not lived up to, and after the former Chief Minister resigned,

Gora approached his successor with similar demands. This led him to arrange talks between Gora and the president of the all-India Congress Party, which again proved to be fruitless.

As the Chief Minister did not show any signs of taking practical steps in accordance with Gora's appeals, a new campaign was launched; this time it was seven days of round-the-clock protest, about twenty volunteers squatting in the scorching sun and soaking rain before the Chief Minister's residence. Some extracts from the diary of one of the satyagrahis give a picture of the atmosphere :

"Punctually at 7–30, the satyagrahis, 19 in number, including three women, marched from 'Gandhi Bhavan', addressing street corner meetings on the way. We arrived at 'Fair Lawns', official residence of the Chief Minister, exactly at 9 a. m. Gora and some police officers greeted each other as old friends, for the officers were on duty during our last campaign as well. But the police also had a duty to perform now. They stopped us a few yards from the gate of 'Fair Lawns'. We squatted on the road. Men and women police lifted us bodily, laid us at the side of the road, and cordoned us off. Mr. K. N. Reddi, chairman of Parakala Municipal Council, came to watch the satyagraha and joined us, making our number 20.

" We obstruct the car of Mrs. Sadalakshmi, the Minister for social welfare, who was visiting Fair Lawns. She got down and walked in. On her return she went to Mrs. Gora and suggested that she take other methods of social welfare than this satyagraha .

"... Later the Chief Minister came to us and in a few straight words asked us to leave the gate clear and sit aside for any length of time. We were astonished at the conduct of our 'First Representative.' We gave up eating for that night in protest against his attitude. Slept on the road beside the gate ..

"The day dawns and we are on the road, cordoned off by the police, and our first representative in that palatial building, guarded by the police. This is the kind of relationship between the people and their representatives in this democraey. Our determination to set the situation right grows in us. Moral weight but not physical force can change this hardened system.

" heavy downpour at midnight. The wife of the Chief Minister sent word twice to keep out of the rain, either by entering Fair Lawns or by taking shelter in the temple, but we said, "No thanks" water falling from above and also flowing from below on the road . a poor man approached us with a petition to be passed on to the Chief Minister as he supposed that we had better access to him . an old decrepit woman who had been waiting for two days to see the Chief Minister explained her woes to us .. for whom is this government? For the few who ride in cars and fight at elections or for the dumb millions who stand in queues at ration shops, like the petitioner and the old woman yesterday?"

This is the spirit with which Gora's Satyagraha Samaj works. As yet they cannot point to any spectacular results of national importance, but the enthusiasm of his workers and the ready response this small group of actionists receives whenever it launches one of its truly Gandhian campaigns is unmistakable and reassuring.

The struggle is hard : as a matter of principle the movement refuses to rely upon financial assistance either from the government or from other established instisutions. To maintain its independence the Samaj carries on entirely on the godwill and sporadic contributions of the people it works among, and these really do not have much to spare. There are no salaries to attract workers, which is perhaps a good thing, as it assures a high quality of idealism and sacrifice, but it is also a drawback in a country where the struggle for existence has first priority.

Still, both through his local and "official" satyagraha campaigns, Gora chips away at intolerable conditions, generating much-needed courage and self-reliance. In a way this movement is providing "the silver voice of truth", independent and bold, so much needed in today's India. It is this fully pledged interpretation of non-violent action which colours all of Gora's thought and action. So, for example, at the time of the Chinese aggression there was no doubt in his mind as to what was the right, even if impractical, course of action. He belonged to the small group of Gandhians who advocated raising a crops of satyagrahis to go to the border, ready to die, if necessary, by Indian bullets.

Unswayed by any pre-set affiliations or vested interests, the Samaj attacks any evils which it sees as endangering the development of what was won by strenuous effort and sacrifice during the freedom struggle. Nothing holds it back, and if Gora and his followers have their way, and are able to overcome the practical obstacless, we may yet see a truly Gandhian revival in free India.

*   *   *

THIS IS GORA

Gora is an all-out revolutionary. He early rebelled against the degrading caste-system, renouncing his Brahmin (highest) caste, leading his family to ostracise him and his wife. He is fighting caste, he is fighting the defeatism and apathy that religion and preoccupation with the other-world has cast on the Indian mind, and as already described, he is fighting the ills in the sphere of politics; all to raise the common man to a realisation of his own dignity and show him the way to a more human existence of freedom and equality. To this end he has adopted voluntary poverty, and from his atheistic centre he carries on caste-mixing programmes, a school for about a hunderd village children, and the various satyagraha struggles in the political field.

Gora, with his ' extreme ' out-look of atheism, equality and direct action, all of a non-violently aggressive character, designed to combat the apathy of the people, has more contacts, true friends and sympathisers than I used to find in more ' moderate ' circles. The reason probably being that he is the first to practise what he preaches, or rather he preaches only what he practises, and the sacrifice and suffering this has carried with it, together with his uncompromising sincerity, make him as irresistable as truth itself.

— Mr. Bjorn Merken in the review of his
one and half years' experiences in India

EXTRACTS FROM GORA'S WRITINGS

WHY ATHEISM?

I was in Calcutta last year. I saw the famine-stricken destitutes walking heavily on the pavements. Here and there some of them dropped dead in the streets. They died beside marts and stalls which exhibited their fruits and sweets for sale. Suppose there was a hungry dog or a bull in the same situation. Would he die of hunger ? No. Beat him, scold him, he would persist in his attempts to pounce upon the shop, somehow eat the sweets and fruits and satisfy his hunger. Why did the destitute not do the same? I do not think they were afraid of the policeman. The destitutes were there in hundreds and thousands. No concerted action was required of them. If a fraction of them had fallen upon the shops, all the policemen in Calcutta put together could not have stopped them. Even confinement in a gaol with its poor diet would have been preferable to death due to starvation. Why, then, did the destitutes not feel desperate and loot the shops? Were they all abject cowards without exception ? Or had all of them such a high sense of civic responsibility as to be unwilling to disturb law and order? No. They were simple, normal folk with no knowledge of civic rights and duties. Had they known their civic rights and duties in the least, there would have been no famine in Bengal at all.

Looking at the other side, were all the shopkeepers so cruel as to allow their fellow-men to die of dire hunger before their own eyes ? No. On the contrary, they shed tears of pity, and contributed liberally and ran the gruel kitchens for the destitutes. They recited hymns of ethics every day.

If the destitute is not cowardly and the shopkeeper is not cruel, why did so many die of hunger? I think the reason is their philosophy of life. Both the shopkeeper and the destitute are votaries of the same philosophy of life. Each one said to himself: " This is my fate, that is his fate ; God made me like this, God made him like that." On account of the commonness of their philosophy, there was no change in their relationship, though some ate their fill and many starved to death. The destitute's faith in that philosophy made his behaviour different from the animal's.

...Man has become worse than the animal. Instead of living well, he is dying ill. His strength to resist evil is very much weakened. The pleasures of the few are built upon the bones of the many. This is really the unhappy fact inspite of our moral professions and pious wishes for the happiness of all humanity. This philosophy of life based upon god and fate – this theistic philosophy – I hold responsible for defeating our efforts at ethical life and idealism.

*   *   *

....Gora said to Gandhiji :

"I could not remove god, if god were the truth. But it is not so. God is a falsehood conceived by man. Like many falsehoods, it was, in the past, useful to some extent. But like all falsehoods, it polluted life in the long run So belief in god can go and it must go now in order to wash off corruption and to increase morality in mankind.

"I want atheism to make man self-confident and to establish social and economic equalities non-violently. Tell me, Bapu, where I am wrong."

Bapuji listened to my explanation patiently. Then he sat up in the bed and said slowly, "Yes, I see an ideal in your talk. I can neither say my theism is right nor your atheism wrong. We are seekers after truth. We change whenever we find ourselves in the wrong I changed like that many times in my life. I see you are a worker. You are not a fanatic. You will change whenever you find yourself in the wrong. There is no harm as long as you are not fanatical. Whether you are in the right or I am in the right, results will prove. Then I may go your way or you may come my way; or both of us may go a third way. So go ahead with your work. I will help you though your method is against mine."

(From "An Atheist with Gandhi")

THEORY AND PRACTICE

Atheism is the opposite of theism. The popular me[a]
of theism is faith in the existence of a god. Though the con[cepts]
of god are many and varied, the quality common to all of th[em]
to regard god as superior to man. Also there are faiths [like]
Hinduism, which do not postulate a god Still they hold [t]
in relentless fate, natural law or something which is de[emed]
superior to man. Therefore in relation to god, fate or law, [man]
stands inferior. The assumption of the inferiority of man s[eems]
more fundamental for theism than belief in god. Thus theis[m is]
evidently the expression of man's feeling of inferiority;
conversely atheism is the expression of man's feeling of free[dom.]

*   *   *

The conflict between theism and atheism is the co[nflict]
between man's slave-mind and his freewill.

*   *   *

An open examination into the nature of god reveals [that]
the concept of god is either a complete falsehood or at be[st a]
hypothesis which is enunciated to explain the meaning of ph[eno]
mena. As god is a postulate supposed by man, its useful[ness]
consists in subserving human happiness But the assumption [that]
god is superior to man smothers man's initiative and fixes hi[m in]
complacent servility.

*   *   *

The slavish submissiveness of the many provides ha[rvest]
for the active few to exploit fellow-men, indeed it is the slave [who]
makes a tyrant of his brother. Consequently, theistic orde[r of]
life seethes with inequalities and injustices, greed and viole[nce]
ignorance and cowardice. The greater the faith the wider th[e]
evils spread.

In order to save the mass of people from the degradat[ion]
into which theism has thrown them, stalwarts with stout heart [like]
Buddha, Jesus, Mohammed, Marx and Gandhi, preached b[y]
action and strong initiative among the common people. Th[eir]
efforts bore fruit. Popular rebellions rose against exploitat[ion]
and enslavement and carried civilisation a step towards comm[on]

weal. It may be that they too talked of god and did not dispense with theistic attitudes altogether. But the new god was so much more rational and revolutionary and so much less deterministic than the old and conventional god that these stalwarts were certainly more atheistic than their contemporaries. By adopting that amount of atheism, they obtained a corresponding amount of progress. They awakened mankind out of former stupor.

*   *   *

Atheistic civilisation is the civilisation of free, equal and moral people. Atheists feel free because atheism is based upon the recognition of the freewill of man. Atheists understand that what are called natural laws and ultimate reality are only interpretations of their experiences. They have no validity except as broad guesses. They shall have to change with evergrowing experiences. Theories can only explain facts. They are neither infallible nor can they contradict facts. As any theory which subordinates man's life to an external control is incompatible with the everyday experience of individual freedom, all theistic theories are wholly false. This understanding should disillusion people with regard to their theistic beliefs.

*   *   *

The greatest contribution of atheism is the provision of a firm basis for ethical conduct. Atheism explains that morality is a social obligaiton but not a passport to heaven and salvation. The theistic belief in divine retribution sidetracked moral behaviour. Believers were more prone to please the god of their imagination by prayer and ritual than to conform to rules of moral conduct. Consequently immorality and anti-social activities spread wild wherever people were absorbed in the worship of god and in the propitiation of fate. Atheism brings about radical changes in the outlook of people in this context Truth, tolerance, love and equality are the basic needs of social harmony. Membership of society imposes on everyone the obligation of their observance now and here. Transgressions should be checked and punished by public opinion and mutual control, since immorality on the part of anyone disturbs the happiness of everyone involved in the social relation. The indirect method of encouraging morality through hope and fear of requitals in the otherworld lent itself to much abuse, especially when the concept of the other-world was exposed to be a big hoax. So atheism which bases morality on social obligation and self-discipline and which controls violations with persuasion and pressure of satyagraha, ensures ethical behaviour more definitely and reliably than religious faith could.

(From "A Note on Atheism")

*   *   *

Theism postulated a creator or a metaphysical reality and subordiated human life to it. But Atheism reveals the fact that the concept of a creator or of an ultimate reality is just man's understanding of the phenomena around him. Man is the creator of the notion of creation and he is the author of the proposition of ultimate reality.

Atheism knows that society is the common understanding between the different members. The common understanding may be increased or decreased at the will of each person...... Society is subordinate to man, but man is not subordinate to society.

By and large, Atheism looks upon man as a master of all situations, which is the opposite of the theistic stand wherein man is deemed to be a slave of god, fate, government, custom or circumstances. When People feel themselves masters, they rise to act and achieve.

... The establishment of equality is the test of atheism.

The individual is the source of all endeavour, he has to shoulder the whole responsibility for his actions. Only when he takes that responsibility does he learn from experience, but the theistic faith tempted him to shove the responsibility for the results of his actions on god, fate or circumstances. The shirking of responsibility has not enabled man to grow wiser than he was in ages past. Otherwise there would not have been untouchability, poverty and war in modern civilisation.

(From the Address at the Atheists' Meet,
January 1970)

HERESY

In, order to be moral an individual must hold himself responsible for his deeds. How can he do so unless he feels free to do or not to do an act? Similarly civilizational progress requires imagination, initiative and effort on the part of individuals. They in their turn require exercise of freewill. So anyone who wanted man to grow more active and more moral necessarily encouraged self-confidence and fellow-feeling. This involved a corresponding discouragement of dependence upon the devotion to god. For instance, look at what Christ said in the Sermon on the Mount :

If thou bring thy gift to the altar and there rememberest that thy brother hath aught against thee, leave thy gift before the altar and go thy way ; first be reconciled to thy brother and then come and offer thy gift. (Matthew 5 : 23, 24)

The above instruction plainly shows how Christ laid greater emphasis on the discharge of moral obligations than the worship of God. There is no wonder that the high priest of the day considered Christ "blasphemous" for such teachings as these (Matthew 26 : 65).

Like Christ, other prophets too had to tread the path of heresy in order to lead humanity towards larger moral behaviour and more kindliness. Heresy may not be the same as open atheism. But undoubtedly every act of heresy is a step taken towards atheism. And the prophets grew more atheistic than their predecessors and contemporaries because they had to contend with the existing faith in god in order to make mankind more free for becoming more moral.

To say that prophets were growing atheistic may appear paradoxical, especially when the last words on the lips of Christ were *Eli, Eli, lama sabachthani* and the last words on the lips of Gandhi were *He! Ram!* (Oh! God Ram!). But it should be noted that there have always been two types of gods : the conventional type and the revolutionary type. The conventional is attributed with more controlling power over man and therefore allows less freedom for human action. The revolutionary type, on the other hand, is regarded as less interfering, and therefore it allows more freedom to man, enabling him to grow more moral. This essential difference between the two types of gods made the devotees of the revolutionary type look atheistic in the view of the devotees of the conventional type. Plato illustrated this important distinction in his account of the trial of Socrates. Meletus, the poet, accused Socrates of corrupting the youth of the city of Athens by teaching atheism. In his dignified defence, Socrates said, "I do believe in God and am not an utter atheist; but only they are not the same Gods which the city recognises. They are different Gods." (Dialogues of Plato, p. 18, Pocket Book edition.) The difference between the two types of gods at any time furthered the atheistic outlook so much that it released freewill sufficient to bring about a revolution in religious faith.

(From "Revolutions in Religions")

DUTY OF A RATIONALIST

Freedom of the individual and equality among people are the two guiding principles for the practice of Rationalism. But equality is a corollary of freedom. If all people act freely, a fair amount of equality prevails among them as they belong to the same species of mankind. Yet the occurence of wide inequalities indicates that all people are not acting with a sense of freedom.

The few people who enjoy freedom, enjoy benefits of civilization also. They live in comfort and luxury. The rest, especially the millions in Asia and Africa, lie downtrodden in want and destitution, because they do not feel that they are free. They think that the course of their life is determined by god, fate, government, social convention, economic order or material circumstances. If these factors were real, they should influence the lives of all people alike, just as sun sheds light where-ever it shines. But the fact that some people feel free and some others feel enslaved proves that the belief in god, government, etc., is a superstitious faith rather than an objective reality. Therefore it is the duty of a rationalist to dispel superstition so that people may feel free and work up for equality.

Material circumstances like wind, rain, sun and soil are, of course, realities. But they are not powerful to mould man's life. On the other hand, civilization consists in man's control of these physical phenomena. The greatness of human life lies in subjugating clime and climate and not in submitting to them.

Unlike the wind and rain, the other factors are not real at all. God, fate, government, convention and property are made and maintained by men as aids for acquiring knowledge for increasing powers of organization and achievement. The aids can be modified or discarded at people's will and pleasure. For instance the form of faith determines the form of god; god goes altogether when people disbelieve in it. Similarly a government derives authority from the cooperation which people give and gathers revenues from the taxes which people pay; if a considerable section of people take to non-co-operation and to non-payment of taxes, any government is bound to collapse. Social convention and private property subsist on people's respect for them. So man is the maker and master of god, government, property and convention. To imagine that he is created by god or that he is a subject of a government betrays only self-deception and servility; practice of rationalism dispels this illusion and liberates people from inferiorities.

Because a rationalist looks at god, government, property, etc., with a sense of freedom, he understands them differently from the superstitious view. To him god is no longer the ultimate reality or the almighty power; god is either a falsehood or at best a hypothesis. So a rationalist is an atheist; politically he becomes a free and vigorous democrat, as a government is only a means of regulating social, ethical and economic relations and it can never be authoritarian. The conception of natural law also loses its relentlessness, it is valid merely as an interpretation of experiences; the form of a law varies with fresh experience and new insight.

By and large, a rationalist feels the master in every situation. He may co-operate with anyone, but he submits to none. A friend but never a slave. Idle complaint has no place in his life; with will and confidence, he steers his life in pursuit of desires. He may not achieve every time whatever he wants. His fellow-men and circumstances influence the course of his life as much as he controls them with the force of his actions. The outcome is the result of the several forces. But his effort is wholly his own, with this effort he not only drives towards the desired end but knows and adjusts the other forces to suit his aim. The fruits of his actions conform to his desires to the extent his endeavour is firm and strong in comparison with other forces. Whereas a superstitious man helplessly drifts, for good or bad, in the stream of circumstances, a rationalist leads a conscious life and directs his way. There is no failure to him ; everything is an experience that enriches knowledge and emboldens further action.

(From "Indian Rationalist", April 1966)

MAN THE MASTER

Indeed the faculty of imagination is the unique feature of human life. Conception of hypothesis and synthesis enriches human knowledge and enables greater achievement. Yet we derive benefit of imagination as long as we know that we are the masters of those concepts; woe befalls us when we become slaves to our own concepts. Concepts of god, government, property, society, nation, universe, natural law and the like aid progress of the knowledge and happiness as long as we treat them as aids. But we fall into prejudice, superstition and war when we submit to them and allow them to dominate our lives. So we save humanity from the evils of hate and violence, if we can persuade people to remember that they are the masters of their concepts.

Atheism banishes slavemindedness and changes the outlook from slavish submission to masterly freedom. A society of free-men is a society in which equality of respect, opportunity and power prevails. So atheists stand up against all types of ignorance, arrogance, oppression and exploitation. Atheism is the need of the age to make man free, bold and moral. I exhort my son to carry the message of atheism and exemplify it in his life.

(From Gora's Message on the Departure of
Lavanam for the United States.)

CAUSALITY

If every thing has a cause and god is the cause of the world, then god also should have a cause and that cause have a cause and so on. But, if it is asserted that god has no cause then it invalidates the original proposition that everything has a cause.

To say that everything has a cause except god is either arbitrary or an indirect admission of the defect of the proposition that everything has a cause.

... The belief that the future is not closed, but that it is open for achievement, is the basis of all our hope, plan and effort at every moment of our life.

But this hope that the future is open is contrary to the belief that everything has a cause.

... A free man is the author of his causes but not their slave.

(*The Atheist, March 1970*)

DEMOCRACY

Open atheism prevents people from slipping into old faiths and ways of life. A permanently awakened mankind is the indispensible condition for the success of socialism and democracy. Only citizens who are activated by the acceptance of atheism can feel the masters of their ministers, can control their government and bend it to serve their needs.

*   *   *

All free people should necessarily live equal too. ... ... And the little variations in taste and form can be accomodated and improved through human sympathy, education and effort. The present distinctions of caste, creed, class, culture, race and nationality among people are maintained partly through a belief that they are divinely ordained and partly through the protection of the barriers with violent force. When people lose faith in divinity, the mischevious ideological sanction behind the distinctions falls into pieces ignominiously. ... ... As the distinctions are removed, the ideal of one humanity and world citizenship comes nearer of realisation.

*   *   *

As an aid to self-discipline, ethical conduct could be regulated by an external agency like a government. When the mass of people were theistically minded and when they were indifferent to the affairs of the government on account of their other-worldly outlook, the institution of a government did enslave and exploit people instead of helping them in the regulation of social behaviour. The attitude will be different when atheism holds the field. The citizens grow realistic, become active and control the government rather than being controlled by it. In as much as a government derives authority from the co-operation which people give and gathers revenues from the taxes which people pay, the government ought to be useful to the people as a servant. So when atheists turn the government to this advantage, it no longer rules but assists people in the maintenance of morality, harmony and equality in social relations. Nevertheless the institution of a government is always attended with the dangers of coercion which are inherent to external control and so it should not only be kept under strict control of the people but its functions should be replaced by self-discipline as soon as possible. Obviously, atheistic outlook with its sense of realism, humanistic approach and active effort is essential for the establishment of good democracy wherein the people govern themselves.

(From "A Note on Atheism")

*　　*　　*

The early method of social organisation was religious belief. It linked up belief in god with the behaviour of man. Good and bad conducts were supposed to receive the blessings and curses of god. The method of religious belief achieved amazing results in keeping man moral. ... Yet the basis of the belief is unsound. ... In the long run religious faith failed to organise society.

The next method which is employed for social organisation is governmental authority. ... Unlike religious faith, governmental authority is real. It collects taxes; it punishes crimes with stripes, fines and prison. It never relates its affairs to beliefs in a being beyod death. Whenever religious faith, on account of its unreality, failed to restrain vice, governmental authority came to its aid even from early times. Priests were known to use cudgels besides curses.

The objective of political power is to punish crime. Crime means anti-social behaviour. All behaviour which raises inequalities in social relations is criminal.

6

Those who exercise governmental authority can coerce people into submission, unless people rebel and control the government. But in early days people were more submissive than rebellious. ... They were indifferent to the real hardships around them. They bore troubles patiently in the hope of a better life beyond death. Political chiefs took advantage of the religious faith of the people. The chiefs claimed the divine right of kings. In the absence of popular protests they could use authority autocratically. Priests and chiefs combined to exploit common people. Consequently the people, who were steeped in religious faith, were impoverished and enslaved. Priests and kings lived in fabulous pomp and luxury, and common people drudged for daily bread.

*   *   *

There are three basic conditions for the success of parliamentary democracy. They are political outlook, equality and small constituencies.

Political outlook in people is the first condition for the success of democracy. It means that people should know that in as much as they pay taxes to a government, the government is the servant of, the people. They should get work done by their government as they get work done by a servant. Of course a part of the work is done by self-discipline and social consciousness of people. This part increases with the increase of self-discipline. But in the course of civilisational progress; our needs and our social contacts have been continuously enlarging, creating tasks which are beyond the capacity of a single individual to accomplish. Formerly people believed that these tasks were fulfilled by divine will. ... ... Political outlook is realistic. It knows that there is no god. So it transfers the responsibility of those tasks from god to government. People with religious outlook prayed to god for the success of their endeavours; people with political outlook insist on their government for accomplishing those tasks. Because religious outlook makes people indifferent to the affairs of their government, political outlook is necessary for people to take interest in their government.

In this way political outlook is atheistic.

The second condition for the success of democracy is equality in economic opportunity and social respect among people.

Without economic and social equalities, the vote cannot maintain the equality of the basic democratic power with which it is invested. In a system of private property, persons with greater economic advantage or with superior social status tend to exercise undue influence over the franchise of the less favoured. The danger is greater, if the legislators enjoy greater economic opportunities. They are already in the possession of greater political power. If they get more wealth too, not only do they treat people with airs of patronage, but the people will be disabled from demanding the right of service of their representatives. The greater pomp of ministers turns democracy completely upside-down. ... Instead of commanding servants to perform their duties, people have to petition to legislators and to ministers to do what is their duty and to give people what is their due. This paradox of democracy can be removed only under conditions of equality. Equality is necessary for the vote to be free at elections and for the citizen to be able to control the legislators.

The third condition for the success of democracy, and particularly of the parliamentary type, is the small size of electoral constituencies. If the constituencies are large, neither the legislators can pay adequate attention to the constituents nor can the people effectively control the legislators. ... Even on account of sheer despair to attend to the needs of a crowd, (the legislator) often represents none but his own interests. After the election a representative cuts himself away from the people of his constituency and plays the game of selfishness. At the time of election too, votes are cast for candidates whom the electors scarcely know. This sad state of affairs weakens the noble purpose of representation which is the very foundation of parliamentary democracy. Therefore representation can be meaningful only when the constituencies are small in size to enable the relationship between the people and their representatives to be close, real and living. The checks and counter-checks between people and their government are possible only when the constituencies are small. Moreover, when the constituencies are small, people can develop intimacy in social relations; they can improve their self-discipline and social consciousness. Consequently, parliamentary democracy can progress towards direct democracy and further towards the condition in which the state could wither away.

PARTY SYSTEM

A political party has the honest, or at least the ostensible intention of providing all people with food and freedom. It has a policy and a programme for achieving the objective. But the method of a party is that it can implement that programme only after capturing the power of the government. So the procedure of a political party boils down to the principle: "Power first, programme next." By power, a party means, the power of governmental authority.

PARTYLESS DEMOCRACY

Partyless democracy means real democracy. Philosophies and constitutions of democracies do not make a mention of parties at all. It is natural. They have to respect the principles of democracy ; and so they cannot associate parties with democracy. Yet, political parties have entered into the working of democracy as conventions outside the constitution.

*   *   *

The political parties, for which there is no provision in the constitution, have cropped up like middlemen, between the powerful government and the ignorant people. ... ... Political parties use their position as middlemen for keeping the people politically ignorant and the government powerful, so that they can gain in the transaction. ... ...

We are caught up in a vicious circle if we think that parties cannot be removed unless people are politically educated, and that people cannot be politically educated unless parties are removed. In order to break the circle, we should take coura e into both hands and start with the establishment of partyless democracy.

Good citizens seldom contest elections and sometimes loathe even to cast votes nowadays. This is a dangerous situation for democracy. If voters outside parties set up candidates whom they consider fit to represent them and also meet the minimum expenses for the contest of elections, persons who deserve to represent people will come forward to bear the responsibility of running democracy.

Whereas party candidates are not able to implement their pledges owing to their involvement in power-politics, partyless candidates will strive for the achievement of their objectives.

Next to elections in democracy is the formation of legislative houses. All the persons who are elected from their respective constituencies are, in principle, representatives of the people only. It was wrong for any of them to have taken up party labels at the election, and worse, if they continue to think in terms of parties even after elections. A legislator represents not only those who cast votes in his favour but also those of his constituency who did not vote for him.

Parliamentary system itself removes democracy a step away from the people, in as much as the representatives of the people govern and not the people themselves. The practice of blocs removes it farther still, as only the majority party governs and not all the representatives of the people. The whipdom degrades democracy to the lowest level. Even in the majority party, it is not the legislators who think and plan, but the party bosses.

The duty of a citizen in democracy is to see that his representative does his duty. ... Obviously simple casting of votes at elections does not constitute domocracy. The voters should exercise check and control all over their elected representatives and see that they behave well.

CAPITALISM

In the modern age the economic problem relates primarily to distribution of wealth rather than to its production. But capitalism impedes distribution. Capitalism encourages pride of possession, even if it means the policy of the dog in the manger. One likes to possess wealth because he has less faith in the friendly help of fellowmen in the hour of need than in bank balances of in material wealth. The economic problem gets solved when the faith in fellowmen increases.

Despite the loud propaganda of Marxists and Gandhians, the common man is not yet thinking in terms of economic equality. Every man desires to get richer. Unlike Marxists and Gandhians, the common man does not want economic equality, but wants to get richer himself in the system of inequalities. Consequently a common man envies the rich but does not hate the rich.

SOCIETY

There is no society apart from the individuals who go to form it. ... Society has no entity. It is a collective concept.

... Because society is a derivative of the individuals, the character of the society depends on the character of the individuals. If the individuals are active and industrious, their society too is active and industrious. If the individuals are superstitious, the society too is superstitious.

... Though the role of the individual in relation to society is so basic and primary, his slave-mind reverses the relation. A slave tends to subordinate himself to something else. Therefore, instead of asserting his individuality and feeling the master of his social relations he, in whom the slave-mind dominates, feels a slave to his society. He thinks that the society is something greater than him and that he is a part of society.

If morality is not observed through self-discipline, it will have to be imposed by social presure. This is the basis of the Gandhian principle of *Satyagraha* (non-violent resistance).

(From *"Partyless Democracy – Its Need and form"*)

ON GANDHI...

In practice, Gandhian ideals boil down to two principles, namely, openness of conduct and active living. Openness ensures non-violence because violence requires secrecy for its hatching. War may seem to be open violence, but its strategy lies hidden deep in secrecy. If the conduct of the belligerents were wholly open throughout, there is no room for the fight of war at all. Emotional outbursts of violence are never so harmful and devastating as violence rooted in secret plan and conspiracy. Just as openness ensures non-violence, active living secures truthfulness. A reasonable inference or an intelligent theory can be truthful in sofar as it conforms to actual living. In short, living is the test of truth. Therefore Gandhi was an activist. As non-violence and truth are moral principles, they are relevant for all time. Gandhi subjected political and economic considerations to .the needs of morality. After Gandhi, Gandhian ideals have suffered a set-back since Gandhians took to secret and sectarian way and deviated from the path of truth and non-violence. Congress, which was a people's movement wedded to the methed of Satyagraha (non-violent resistance), became a sectarian political party after Gandhi's assassination. Nevertheless Gandhian ideals can be restored to their vigour and glory if the method of Satyagraha is again taken up.

(The Atheist, June 1969)

MARX AND GANDHI

Marxism has recourse to political dictatorship for achieving economic equality. Gandhism played into the hands of reactionary elements, because Gandhi used theistic language to explain atheistic methods. Despite their honest efforts neither of them could awaken the mass of mankind from their habitual apathy and indolence, because they did not openly preach atheism.

(From the address at the Atheists' Meet,
January 1970)

WOMEN

Lust is as powerful an instinct as hunger. Just as private property restricted wealth to a few rich and deprived the rest of food, the custom of marriage restricts the satisfaction of lust to those who are married and deprives the unmarried of the facility to satisfy their lust. Further, just as secret ways of theft become necessary for the poor to satisfy their hunger, as long as the respect for private property lasts, secret ways of adultery and fornication become necessary for the unmarried to satisfy the needs of lust, as long as the respect for marriage remains.

By and large, the problem of unmarried mothers calls for an immediate change in our outlook. As long as the institution of marriage lasts for its own advantages, unmarried mothers should be treated with respect equal to married mothers. ... ...

The change should be both ways. The public should cease to talk opprobiously of unmarried mothers; also unmarried mothers should not consider their condition shameful.

50

An open rebellion against private property put an end to theft; an open rebellion against the sanctity of marriage will render adultery meaningless.

The problem (of unmarried motherhood) relates only to women on account of their structural difference with men. O ˙ account of the absence of the womb in men, they escape the shame to which women are put for the same act. Man's claim of impunity is as unjust as white man's claim of superiority over the dark-skinned.

(The Atheist, July 1969)

*　　*　　*

Common people rest content with worshipping great men instead of adopting their way of life.

Mr. Gora wields an indefatigable pen
in the cause of atheism.

— The New Zealand Rationalist & Humanist.

SWATANTRA ART PRINTERS, VIJAYAWADA-4